Our Lady's Unknown Mysteries

Catherine Doherty

MADONNA HOUSE PUBLICATIONS
Combermere, Ontario, Canada

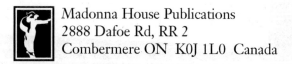

Madonna House Publications
2888 Dafoe Rd, RR 2
Combermere ON K0J 1L0 Canada

www.madonnahouse.org/publications

Our Lady's Unknown Mysteries
by Catherine de Hueck Doherty

First Edition: Dimension Books, 1979

2nd edition: Madonna House Publications, 1991

3rd Printing: August 2010

Printed in Canada

Cover Art by Marysia Kowalchyk, *Our Lady of Tenderness*.

Library and Archives Canada Cataloguing in Publications

Doherty, Catherine de Hueck, 1896-1985
Our Lady's Unknown Mysteries / Catherine de Hueck Doherty. — 3rd Printing

ISBN 978-0-921440-19-2

   1.   Mary, Blessed Virgin, Saint – Poetry. I. Title

BT608.5.D65 1990   C811'.54   C90-090308-2

This book is set in Janson Text, designed by Nicholas Kis of Hungary in about 1690. Its strong design and clear stroke contrast combine to create text that is both elegant and easy to read. Headings are set in University Roman, from the Charleston Collection.

Dedication

To Mary, who is always with me, awake or asleep.

CONTENTS

Introduction vii

The Seven Unknown Joys of Mary.. 1

    The First Joy 3
    The Second Joy 11
    The Third Joy 15
    The Fourth Joy. 19
    The Fifth Joy 23
    The Sixth Joy 27
    The Seventh Joy. 31

The Seven Unknown Sorrows of Mary 35

    The First Sorrow 37
    The Second Sorrow 43
    The Third Sorrow 51
    The Fourth Sorrow 57
    The Fifth Sorrow 63
    The Sixth Sorrow. 69
    The Seventh Sorrow 75

The Seven Unknown Glories of Mary 83

    The First Glory 85
    The Second Glory 91
    The Third Glory 99
    The Fourth Glory 107
    The Fifth Glory 115
    The Sixth Glory. 125
    The Seventh Glory. 133

    About the Author 139

Introduction

Our Lady's Unknown Mysteries is one of the simplest yet most profound of Catherine Doherty's writings. It consists of meditation, poetry, prose, and prayer, written over a period of time and combined into a whole.

It was formed in the silence of Catherine's heart, a silence of deep union with Mary, whom she always loved. Catherine entered into this silence and came to know the Mysteries which she later unfolded for us on the pages of this book. We read of Mary's soul-searching Sorrows, her hidden Joys and Glories, as we have not known them before.

Catherine did not merely 'have a devotion' to Our Lady. She possessed a treasure of immeasurable value—a deep and abiding relationship with Mary. For Catherine, this was *a way of life!* Mary was her constant companion, her closest friend, a true Mother. Mary was the one to whom she turned, without condition or reserve, allowing Mary to form Jesus within her, and to lead her on 'the path of the Gospel' in all that she did.

Many of these Mysteries were written long before the events of history began to confirm, as they do now, the prophetic nature of Catherine's vocation. She lived as a noblewoman in Russia, was a refugee from the Revolution of 1917, and arrived in North America virtually penniless. She rose again to riches, only to hear the call of Jesus to forsake everything and follow him.

She devoted the rest of her life to the service of the Gospel 'in the poor.' In and through all of this, she was led to a unique position in which to receive these Mysteries and to pass them on to others. When she died in 1985, Catherine left behind a spiritual legacy which is only now beginning to be tapped.

"A mystery.
Quietly She makes Her way
Into the poorer parts of town,
Of city streets and rural roads.
All know Her soft and holy tread well,
For our Lady is about the business of
Her seventh unknown joy in glory –
THE LOST FORGOTTEN LONELY SOULS
That loved Her, notwithstanding all the darkness
And weight that pressed them down."
(excerpt from the Seventh Joy)

The Seven Unknown Joys of Mary

The First Joy

The stone rolled off,
    And no one saw it.
Her heart was jubilant
And full of ecstasy.
She knew that a sea of joy
Would flow out of the sea of sorrow;
Although it would
Recede to sorrow again.

She could remember
Being born in the midst of
God the Father,
And being created
Before creation.
Did She truly watch
Light come out of darkness?
Did she see shores
Come into being?
It seemed you could play
See-saw on a wave!!

She never moved.
Quietly and closed in a room,
She sat behind a door
That no one dared to open,
And looked upon the streets
Of Her beloved Jerusalem,
Watching the crowds
Hurrying hither and yon;
Watching, and not seeing at all;

For the sea of sorrow
Was receding
Into the desert
Where seas go;
And She was playing
See-saw on a wave
Made by God.

She knew the Pieta was Piety.
The sorrow in her face
Was sorrow of the past.
Upon it lingered still
The shadow of the cross
And Him upon it;
But when Her hands
Had touched His face,
Which the disciples thought was dead,
She felt the warmth
Pulsating through it.
How could God die?

He touched death
For an instant—
Abolished it forever,
And it became
An angel of surpassing beauty,
For whom men of faith
Would wait with bated breath;
Death hasn't icy fingers at all
They are warm—
The fingers of the angel of love.
The ice, the cold, the decay
That is for men of earth to see;
For their eyes are not conditioned
To the resplendent state of the soul.

She knew
He was not dead forever;
Not one bone would decay.
He slept, quietly, obediently,
In the tomb;
For He was obedient
Even after death.

But when they rolled
The stone before the tomb
He was free to roam;
To come, to go
To be
Where all those years
He could not be
Or could not show Himself.

Out of the tomb
To hell,
To bring joyous news;
Then, like a man
Would visit
In a pilgrimage of love,
The places
That made His heart
Beat faster
As a man.

When She had held His cold-warm body
She trembled
With the joy of it—
Knowing He would come
To visit Her first
The Magdalene would be next
To see Him.

So She sat alone
With the door closed—
They thought to grieve.
But no! To wait.
Who was there to see
Or hear what passed?
Who was there to know
The glory
Of music born in that room?
The music of His voice and Hers
Mingling as voices
Never did before.

"Tonight is the night
Of my first unknown joy.

"It is just as well
That men count them as seven;
For how else could they count
My joys or sorrows?
There are not enough stars
In heaven
To add them up—
My sorrows, joys, and glories.
For the weak eyes of men
Seven will do nicely.
Come;
Share
In one of
My unknown joys.

"He came to Me
In My chamber,
My Son!
My Lover!
And overflowing rapture,

Condensed in utter ecstasy,
Filled Me again.

It was as if
I had conceived anew,
For all My being
Felt His coming.
The room pulsated
With the beat
Of angels' wings
But even the seraphs' eyes
Were sealed.
Not even they
Could look then
Upon the Mother and the Son.
And so they chanted
Alleluias.

"Did you know that I,
The first stigmatic,
Had the wounds?
It happened simply,
Perhaps He was two or three,
Perhaps, I am not sure.
It is hard
For one who encompasses eternity
To think in time.
One day He was playing
At My feet,
And suddenly,
Like a little swallow
He kissed each foot.
The wounds
Began to throb.

"At seven or eight
He kissed each palm,
Lingeringly.
And I knew
The feel of nails.

"He came once
In early spring,
On a shiny sunny day.
His hands were full of flowers.
He sat on a small stool
And wove a crown for Me.
I knew the feel and weight
Of thorns
Upon My head.

"In May, in your land,
Children repeat His gesture.
It brings back the memory
Of thorns, sweet, deep, sharp.

"He was a suckling at My breast.
One night,
Somehow, His face fell
From My nipples;
And His warm mouth
Touched my side.
Was it a kiss?
Was it a lance?
From that blest night
The pain was there
Never to go.

"So you must know
My unknown joy,
The rendezvous We held—
My Son and I—

The night they thought
They had sealed His tomb
So tight.
Where do you think
He went?
He went to the place
He loved most in Palestine—
The room of His Mother.

"Wonders will never cease!!
The room was aflame;
For where My Son is,
There is My spouse,
The Crimson Dove
Who holds Me tight.
The angels' wings
Made melody of strings,
As they chanted their
Alleluias
In a circle of bliss.
And He sat at My feet,
And I looked into His eyes—
Above to below.

"The Crimson Dove
Brought the flame of love;
And the Father was there
Unseen, jubilant, joyous,
Taking delight in His Son.
And as He did,
The Crimson Dove grew,
And a flame covered the earth.
Alleluia
Alleluia
Alleluia.

"The stone was still tight
On the tomb of My child
Who was with Me.

"I give you the Paschal gift.
Put out your hands
And take it to your heart
This is the night of joy!
Alleluia!
I am an
Alleluia
In the flesh
Tonight."

The Second Joy

Glory unending!
Trembling,
I, the Mother of God, stood before it
Unbound, perfect,
In the glory of Him
Who came to earth to Me.
Lights indescribable,
Gold, silver, melting,
Cascading around,
Diamonds strewn about,
All reflecting in a thousand ways
The sun of the face
That no mortal can see!

Standing before its majesty,
Looking into the eyes of the Father,
I was lost
In a glory that surpasses all glory
Known to angels and men.

Spirit uncreated,
Infinite,
All-seeing,
All-loving,
All-comprehending,
Unencompassable,
From Whom stems light,
Eternally immovable,
Fecund just in being,
From Whom all paternity flows

Like a river,
Creative of body and soul.

Three rivers depart from this Spirit;
Three rivers of paternity
That flow over all that is.
From its creativeness came in an instant
That which was not;
Motionless, motion,
Begetting by thought,
Encompassing all of spirit and being,
Lifted without an effort
Into the center of it
And returned to the Triune Glory.

Glory begetting glory.
And I, a woman of earth,
Lifted up,
Found myself lying in the arms of my Spouse,
The Crimson Dove;
Crowned by the Father and the Son,
And loved by the Father.
Spirits that were motion,
(And so men would call them Angels)
Were forming a carpet
On which the Queen of Angels
Might rest the tips of Her toes
While She nestled
In the wings of the Dove
Regina coeli!

Heaven is everywhere;
For where God is, love is,
And God is everywhere.

I am held
In the glory of the Three,

But free
To go where love sends me.
Mediatrix of all graces!
The Father looks.
The Dove holds.
The Son bends
And crowns my head!
Triune in One encompass me.
All their graces enter me
As once His Seed did;
For graces are the
Seeds of eternal glory.

She who received the seed of eternal glory
Now dispenses grace, the seed of glory-to-come.
My womb was the chalice of the impenetration of God
That became the Incarnation of God and man.
Glory unending,
Light uncreated,
Infinite might,
Expresses Itself in light.
And light is life,
And life is love.

I stand,
And through me
The light pours,
Life enters,
And love goes forth.
I am the Mediatrix of all graces—
Light, Life, Love,
Depths, heights,
Horizons unending.

Cruciform,
In the middle
Mediating

Is Mary
The Mother of God,
To Whose heights no creature scaled,
Whose depths no creature knew.

MY GLORY WAS MY SECOND JOY—
Though my Crowning is well known.

My slaves and sons are men of peace,
And so—
Come to my gates
When they feel
The scratching of the foe.

The Third Joy

Queen of Saints!
The third unknown Joy
Of Mary in glory.

What does
The Mother of the Crucified feel
When She looks into
The souls of saints?
"The perfume of beauty encompasses Me
From the souls of the saints.
I walk in fragrance
And so does He.
Do you know the stench of sin,
Of death and decay?
If you did
You would understand
The third unknown joy
Of Mary.

"It is the hearts and minds and souls
Of Saints;
And mirrored in them
Is the beauty
In which I live.
They tremble with love
At His name.
Their prayers are like
The wings of white birds
That come to nestle
Around His wounded heart;

Like the wings of bees
Keeping it cool;
Like the fluttering kisses
Of a little child
That runs to his mother.

"They bring joy to the heart
Of My Son.
And He smiles
And all heaven
Smiles with Him.
And the Father's benediction
Falls on the souls of the saints;
And the fragrance intensifies
And covers Me and My Son,
And He reposes in it
Like a bridegroom
On the breast of His bride.

"Day by day,
Minute by minute,
The saints weave
A seamless garment
For My Son;
Shimmering with a thousand colors;
Filled with tears
Shed and unshed;
Colored threads,
Words unspoken,
Thoughts unthought,
Obedience,
Trust,
All held tight—
Woof and warp
Of this seamless garment.

"Day by day,

Night by night,
Hour by hour,
Threads of white,
Red, blue, green,
All converging
All golden
With love.
Behold My Son
Bending down
And clothing Himself
In the garments of love,
Behold Him rising
In the splendor
Of a responding love.
Creature loving God:
God loving back!"

THE SOULS OF THE SAINTS,
This is the third unknown Joy
Of the Queen of Saints,
Mary,
The Mother of God.

"Give My Son saints.
We need saints
For My Son is so sad
These days.
Give me saints
To console My Son with,
And to give food
To My third unknown Joy."

The Fourth Joy

Tender, bruised, tired,
  Walking through the dust of many roads,
The Fourth-Joy-In-Glory of Our Lady appears.
Strange, unfathomable,
Yet simple, like Herself,
The Mother of all men,
The fourth joy approaches slowly.
Feet, stained with the dust of a thousand roads,
Garments torn by strange highways—
Always side roads, and
Wrong turnings at crossroads—
All have left their mark on the feet and garments of
The fourth unknown joy of Mary.

Immense, yet small,
Head bowed down,
Hands folded on breast,
Or like a chalice,
Holding the tears shed,
Hair streaming, strangely fine,
Yet uncombed,
The sounds of the fourth joy
That She seems to wish to hide from the eyes of all.

Hair whipped by rain, storm,
Tangled by cold, heat,
Matted from lying wherever the tired feet fell,
Smelling of sea and campfires,
Still holding in its silken strands
The perfumes of the world left behind—
THE FACE OF A SINNER REPENTANT!

Slowly yet steadfastly she nears;
Wounded yet not afraid
Hair covering her sores,
She comes.

And She, The Queen of Apostles and Martyrs,
She, abiding in the crooked wings of the Crimson Dove,
Reflecting unseen the face of God the Father,
She, descending, plummeting
Like a star—
To land as soft as a feather
In the dust of a thousand roads—
Is running, light as a child after a butterfly,
To cover with Her blue mantle (now resplendent
With the gems of the treasure chest of God)
The face of a sorrowing sinner!

Repentant sinners do not know the glory
That covers the Woman who waits for them.
They run, stumble, fall at Her feet.
They see only a mother,
And washing Her feet with their tears,
They call out—
"Oh, Mother!"

Gently, She lifts up the tangled hair.
Lo and behold! It shines.
The uplifted face of the repentant sinner,
Cupped in Her hands,
Becomes one that the angels must veil their faces
To look at.

The resounding joy of Heaven,
The Alleluia, the Gloria,
Merge in a symphony
Unknown and unheard on earth!

Thin, like a flute,
Yet suddenly hushing all the other voices,
Is heard the song of the Virgin Mother.
And then like a mighty organ,
The choirs of angels thunder their Alleluias!
As the Mother of God
Takes the repentant sinner
Into the heart of Her Son.
And as She beholds His face shining,
She, standing on a carpet of angels' wings,
Dressed in a splendour unknown on earth,
Rejoices in Her Fourth Joy—
To bring a repentant soul
To assuage the thirst of Her Son.
Alleluia.

The Fifth Joy

Whiter than snow in the north,
  Unseen and unwalked by man;
Whiter than Communion veils;
Whiter than hosts, consecrated by the hands of a priest;
Whiter than the crest of the wave—
Whiter is Mary's robe.

She stands in midst of gold that shines
around the throne of God.
The white reflects the light
And becomes whiter still.
She stands in the midst of the splendour that surrounds the
    throne of God.
What color is splendour?
Touch the hem of Her robe.

Behold the Immaculateness of the Mother of God.
Glory and love that can not be told—
In the midst of it all,
Whiter than the host consecrated by the hands of a priest,
Stands the Immaculate Mother
Of the Virginal Son.

She comes, this way, towards us,
Clothed in white.
Stars make a pathway
For the Queen of Angels and men.
Fragrance indescribable
Surrounds Her.
Stars get heady and dance with the joy of it.

Because of Her priests.

The fifth joy of Our Lady in glory
Is the SOUL OF A PRIEST
Who has forgotten all things of the world
And lives in the heart of God.
The Fifth Joy and glory of Mary
Is the heart of such priests.

Behold the Queen of heaven
Descending the golden way
Of golden stars.
Behold her stepping and bending over a priest at a time.
See Her arms upholding a veil
That is whiter than white
Brighter than bright,
Iridescent,
That reflects the throne of the Almighty,
And the red of Her Son's heart,
And the wings of Her Spouse,
Behold Her lifting the veil
Behold Her covering with its whiteness
The priests.

Behold Her two small hands
Uplifting such priests
Right to the bosom of Him, the
Immense, Uncreated,
God the Father,
And He bends a little toward Her
And into His arms paternal
He takes the priest,
And, with a smile, returns him
To the Mother of men
And the Queen of all priests.
Her hands lower the priest gently,

And he stands from where She took him.
He is filled with zeal
And a glory he does not know!
But all those whose eyes are unsealed
Know, and veil their eyes.

The hands of the Almighty
Have touched no one but His Son;
And each priest through Mary
Is Her Son.

The fifth joy is the souls of such priests
As She can bring to the throne of the Almighty.
Behold Her covering the earth,
Stopping before big cathedrals and little shacks.
Unerringly, She discovers those who love Her Son.
And then She returns to heaven
On the same golden way of stars.

How white Her whiteness!
How perfect Her robe!
And yet, shimmering strangely
At the hem here and there,
Is a diamond glistening
That was not there before.
Oh, No! They are the tears of Her priests.
She embodied them to bring to the Kingdom.

All priests who love Her Son
Through tears of loneliness, and
Through dreary days,
Are gems to remind Her
Of Her fifth Unknown joy
In the glory of God.

The Sixth Joy

Red—lining a mantle blue.
Red—never seen on earth.
Blood reflecting the Crimson Dove.
Cardinal red.
Red of human blood divinised.
Divine red is the color
That lines the mantle of blue.
And the blue is not blue—
It has shades
That are almost pale white
And reflect the blue of the sky at night;
Or the blue of the sky in the day;
Or the blue of the eyes of a child at play;
Or the blue of a flower
That God created yesterday
To gather all the blues
From the first day to this.
Every blue everywhere is reflected
In the blue mantle
Lined with red.

The hair is unbraided,
Cascading down;
A mantle over a mantle.
Brown with gold, not black,
Catching the lights
Of all the stars, the sun and moon,
But mostly catching the eyes of the Son
And reflecting them back
In the eyes of the Father—
Such is the color of Mary's hair.

Slowly, floating on nothing at all,
Or maybe just walking on air—
(Why not?
Peter walked on the sea;
Mary walks on air.)
As angels uphold her,
And air caresses
Her little toes,
Demurely and slowly
She descends
Like a princess a staircase.

There is grace in every movement,
And the eyes seek out something
On the earth.
There is no haste in Her steps
There is slowness and sureness,
As if She knew
Where She was going,
And why and how.
And why shouldn't She?
She is about to touch the sixth joy in Her glory.
And that is
THE SOULS OF MYSTICS.

For them She cherishes a special love.
On each She lavishes the care
That a Mother gives the Bride of Her Son.
Notice how gently She walks, not to distract
The souls asleep in the arms of God.
How well does She know
The weakness of men
And the fears
That beset such souls!
See how gently She walks
As She smiles and bends
Over a soul

In the torments of love;
How soothing Her hands
As She gathers from each
Their love for Her Son,
And makes a chaplet of each!

That is the Rosary our Lady tells.
Look at it shimmering, burning in Her hands.
Understand?
That is the Psalter
Our Lady says
To Jesus Christ,
Who stretches out His hands
And holds them
Beneath this iridescent chaplet,
And catches
The beads
As they fall
From Mary's hand.

The sixth joy
Is the chaplet
She gathers anew every day
And brings back to heaven with Her
As She walks, gracious, majestic,
Over Her stairway of air.
Chaplet by chaplet
She lays them at the feet of God the Father.
He is quite pleased to see
Such gracious beads
That lie so still at His feet
And glow with such love for His Son.
The Crimson Dove approaches,
And, with tip of His wing, touches them!

The souls of the mystics
That form the chaplet

Glow ruby red
From the kiss of the Dove!

Behold!
Her mantle lined with red
Becomes alight
As She again descends, stately and gracious,
To seek for more mystic souls
To bring Her Son.

When night falls
She comes back and lays the mystic souls
On Her lap,
And plays with them,
The beads
As a child would
She takes great joy in them,
As does Father, Son and Holy Spirit
Who watches Her play.

After a while
She sends them back;
And that is when you see the mystics
Grown in wisdom and grace and love
Of Her Son.
What else could happen
To any mystic soul
That lay at the Father's feet,
Was touched by the Holy Spirit
And then went back to earth?
What else could happen to the souls
That furnished the Queen of the Rosary
Her sixth unknown joy?

The Seventh Joy

Clad in working clothes, as in Nazareth,
Her feet in sandals,
Her hair unbraided
But, underneath the veil
Tied with a heavy ribbon
To hold it back;
Graceful and light,
Our Lady, who delights
The eyes of countless angels,
Descends quietly
Over a terrace
Like a stairway of clouds,
That tremble
And hold Her lightly
In their mist-like, delicate embrace.

Her Jewish work-day clothes
Seem to blend with every age and clime.
She fits even
In our present year of grace.
The inconspicuousness of it is strange,
A mystery.
Quietly She makes Her way
Into the poorer parts of town,
Of city streets and rural roads.
All know Her soft and holy tread well,
For our Lady is about the business of
Her seventh unknown joy in glory—
THE LOST FORGOTTEN LONELY SOULS
That loved Her, notwithstanding all the darkness

And weight that pressed them down.

Now behold Her
In front of a Salvation Army Hostel,
A place for men called derelicts.
How gently She approaches this or that one.
Presently her dark mantle
Has covered one;
And up flies a soul
Wrapped snugly in its folds.
That mantle is a passport to Saint Peter's gate.
Who would dare to stop
A soul wrapped in it?

Mystery of mysteries!
There She is on a park bench,
Wrapped in the same mantle
That just flew upwards, covering a soul,
Talking to an old and toothless prostitute
With crookedly rouged lips and crinkly hair,
One still trying to ply her trade
Of love that is not love.
And now the bluish, pallid
Ill-smelling
Clumsily rouged mouth
Has the sweetest smile;
And the tired head
Rests on Our Lady's shoulder.

Police pronounced the woman dead,
But choirs of angels know she lives.

—And so to other streets—
Bending over a tired mother;
Caressing a cripple's face;
At a street corner lifting up a drunkard.
And at the end of all streets—shantytown,

Even in shantytown,
She is at home.

Slowly wending Her way
Through a world of twilight,
Darkness, poverty, and ruin,
Our Lady gathers Her seventh joy—
The souls that loved Her
 In the darkness
Of the inhumanity
That men can show to men;
The souls that still remembered
To say, once in a while,
The Hail Mary,
Or just to invoke Her
By Her first name—
Mary.

At eventide She will return—
The resplendent Mother of God
Dressed in an ordinary
Jewish woman's working clothes
That blend miraculously
With every age and clime
And even enter our present year of grace—
At eventide She will return
To Her heavenly domain.

She will walk to the corner,
Just inside the gate,
Where Peter has laid out
All souls
Wrapped in the simple dark mantle
She put on them.
Behold Her,
Smiling at all Her treasure
With tender love!

She seems to lift them all at once
And lay them at the throne of God.
No words pass between
Her and Her Son
They just look
Into each other's eyes
As they did on earth
During His Passion.
He smiles and bends,
And invites each one of them
To sit
At the right hand of the Father.

He understands—
The Man Who saw the eyes
Of Mary
On His way to Golgotha—
He understands
That Her name on human lips
Is a key
To heaven's gate.

Our Lady smiles,
And all heaven is radiant with joy,
For our Lady's seventh joy—
The souls that held on to Her
Throughout their pitiful and broken lives.
The souls are there to stay
And She rejoices in them. Amen.

The Seven
Unknown
Sorrows of Mary

The First Sorrow

Alone in heaven
Where all is joy—
She cries.
Black is Her dress
Against the white
Of angel wings.
They stand in silence
Awed, and still,
Before Her who alone can weep
In heaven where no one knows tears.
One by one they fall
Into the chalice
Finely-wrought of gold.
Or is it gold?
It seems to be incredibly transparent
As if one could see through it.

The same immense and awesome angel
Who, once on earth, prostrated,—
Called her "FULL OF GRACE"
Holds this chalice strange,
Wrought by no earthly hands.
The immense spread of his wings,
That are not wings at all,
Desires to protect.
He holds the chalice of strange transparency
Where the tears fall;
A treasure beyond compare.

Kept there by whom? For what?
Slowly, dressed in black,
Her face as white
As when She stood
Beneath the cross of Him
Who was Her Son
In flesh alone—
For earthly Father He had none—
She descends
On Gabriel's wings
That, gently holding up the chalice
For the tears that weigh so heavily,
Yet make a stairway for Her,
Unseen yet firm,
From heaven back to earth.

What is this?
Our Lady's tears
Flow fast.
She stands before a house
That looks like any house
At all anywhere,
In a year of grace.
Suddenly She straightens out,
Weary, as if the weight
Almost crushes Her.
Yet She has to go on.
Slow, hesitant, tired Her step.
She enters through a door
Into a room.
There is a man there
Before him She stands,
Unseen but not unfelt.
His head comes up.
He listens as if he had heard
Some distantly remembered steps;

Over his face move
Astonishment, disbelief and scorn.
Lightly She lays Her hand upon his brow.
He stiffens
And throws it off
In a motion of hatred and despair,
Rejection, pride defiant and complete.
Our Lady backs against the wall,
And Gabriel shivers outside the door.
His form, immense, takes on another hue.
No longer is he the humble angel.
Immense, avenging,
Held only by obedience,
He shows the power given spirits like him.
And, descending like an arrow,
Michael stands beside his fellow angel,
Holding himself in readiness.

But our Lady,
With arms flat against the wall,
Has not moved
There is no fear
In Her posture;
Only an infinite and heart-breaking sorrow.
O Mater Dolorosa!
Why are you here?
The angels veil their faces—
(They haven't any;
Yet they have.)
Michael trembles,
Gabriel gathers himself.

O Mater Dolorosa!
Why are you here?
There is no answer
From the Woman wrapped in silence
With Her arms against the wall.

She stands as one in torment
And slowly, tears
Like diamonds, fall
Down her cheeks
To the floor at the man's feet.
But oh! the light
That comes
From them as they touch the dark drab carpet!
It is intolerable
To Michael and Gabriel.
Their wings have dropped,
As if they were about to die.
(But angels know no death.)

O Mater Dolorosa!
Why are you here?
There is no answer;
But suddenly
The room is strangely silent,
The darkness of a sort falls into it.
Impossible!
On an ordinary street
In the United States or Canada
In a year of grace.
Oh No! No!
The man, though sitting,
Stands
And lo!
There are shadows in the room;
As if men were sitting
At a long elaborate table,
And one was slowly
COUNTING OUT
Thirty pieces of heavy silver!

The man at the table
has not moved,
Yet he walks,
And into his hands
Are falling
Thirty pieces of heavy silver!

Why are they so red?
But this is an ordinary street!
The man is dressed like many other men.
Sport shirt, trousers, shoes.
But as he holds out his hands
For the silver,
He is suddenly dressed in black.
His collar is a Roman collar.
HE IS A PRIEST!!

The angels lie prostrate
On the porch.
Michael is shaken;
Gabriel weeping.
The Woman in silence stands
Against the wall
And watches the silver pieces falling
Into the hands
Of a priest of God!

But what is this?
The silver is not silver,
Confusion, power, lust—
So many things can look like
Thirty pieces of silver.
They don't have to be thirty heavy Roman coins;
They can be anything
That a man makes an idol of
In the depths of his soul
And sells God for.

And now
The Woman with tear-stained face
Walks out the door
And leaves a man in sport shirt, trousers, shoes
(In the United States or elsewhere)
Sitting by a table,
In a dark, chill room.
And slowly
On the trembling wings of Gabriel and Michael
All night
Mary
Tries to win back
To Christ
The fallen-away priest
But she comes back to heaven
Without a soul.
That is Her first unknown sorrow.

You who pass by,
Help Her in Her search
Pray for priests
That they may remain
With Peter—or better, with John,
And whisper to them
That even though they have sold Him,
To cry out "Rabboni."
Then, like a star descending,
His Mother will be at their side
And they will enter into Her joys.

It is a terrible thing
To make
The Mother of Fair Love
Shed tears
Where no one else can—
In heaven—At the feet of God!

The Second Sorrow

Slow, like a dirge;
Moving, beating,
Chanting its song of pain,
The heart of the Immaculate
Weeps in Her bosom,
As She wafts down from heaven
Like a dark veil.
As She passes,
Stars are dimmed in pain;
The moon trembles,
And the sun,
Wherever it may be, hides
Behind the blackest cloud
That it can see.

She falls, and lies,
Seemingly like a broken thing,
At the feet of the Man in White,
In the City called holy,
The stones of which
Cry with gladness
Because they were washed
With martyrs' blood
And felt the flesh
Of many saints
Upon their ancient surfaces.

She breathes with infinite pain.
One would think
That the young Queen of Heaven

Carried all the weight of the years
Since God created time.
Her every movement
Sings of pain and weariness,
And hints of
All the unshed tears
Her soul holds
With a clutch
Of tragic sorrow.

The Man in White
Is praying
Before Her Son.
He doesn't see
That the black veil
Lying at his feet
Is not a veil
But the Mother of Jesus Christ.

He does not see
The slow rising of the Immaculata,
His face is buried
In his hands,
And man that he is
He groans.
A weight is placed
On the shoulders
Of the Man in White
And stains them crimson.

And now She stands
Erect, mobile,
Again our Mater Dolorosa.

There is no cross.
This is not Palestine.
It is just a chapel

On the Holy Hill
Called the Vatican,
Where the Man in White
Prays to Her Son,
Because he is
His ambassador on earth
In fact—Himself.

This is not Palestine
But Rome,
In a year of grace.
And yet the Immaculata
Is carved
In the stillness of Her pain.
And suddenly
There are no walls at all.
They vanish.
The Man in White still prays.
But She who stands so still
That you would take Her for a statue,
Observes the world
As on a screen.

Slowly, much of it fades away,
And in a light
That comes from somewhere,
One cannot say from where,
This figure or that is pinpointed.
Each time one comes into focus
The Immaculata lifts up Her hands
And folds them
On Her slowly beating Heart.
And tears roll out
From the eyes
Of God's Mother
And hang there, poised,
As if afraid to crush the earth
Should they descend on it.

Pinpointed in the light—
It is from hell or heaven?—
Majestically clad in red, are
Cardinals, Archbishops, Bishops—
Figures moving slowly as on a screen.

Here is one of the princes of the court
Of the Divine Pauper
Who makes himself
Quite comfortable in an overstuffed chair.
There is about him an air of grandeur, pride,
Surely he's nobody's fool.
Urbanely he hobnobs with the mighty
And talks of buildings, mortgages, percentages, incomes;
In blocks, he buys, on the tips of friends, and strangers
That curry the favor of his power.
In blocks he buys, Bell Telephone, Bethlehem Steel,
Or other values.
"After all, one has a position to maintain."
Two tears fall
From the eyes of the Madonna
And join the first in mid air.

The light moves
And pinpoints another room,
Another figure
Clad in the same shade of red.
"O damn nonsense, I don't want to be troubled
with such trash. Keep your feet on the ground.
After all, the Pope doesn't know this country.
The laity indeed! Bread and meat, the Sacraments,
short homilies if you can squeeze one in.
Let's have order in this diocese, and be done
with all that riff-raff. What was good enough
for our fathers is good enough for us. I
declare the need of several million dollars for

bigger things. The Negro? It's too early to
try radical procedures. No, Fathers, none of
this; just keep to the clear outline I gave you,
and don't get the diocese in any trouble with
all that flimsy and foreign stuff.   Hmmmm,
a priest contaminated with that Vatican II
stuff. I'll have to do something about it.
The Pope is really getting senile..."

The head of
The Man in White
Bows lower.
Two more tears
Fall from
The eyes of
The Mother of God
And join the others.
There is the beginning
Of a necklace there!
But woe to them
Who had part
In making this necklace.

A third figure
Moves in to the light:
"Let's compromise; let's keep the status quo;
let's apply human reason to these things—
we'll give in to this and that; yes, the politician
should stay in his post; a little scandal;
well, just cover it up. But we must make our
way and get ahead as Catholics. The bus question
we'll shelve; and by all means, don't touch the
Negro. You know, I really believe in this
Machiavellian stuff."

Lower falls
The head of the Madonna.

Two more tears fall
And join the others.

Then the light falls on
The supine,
The indifferent,
On those
Who like
What goes with the red.
And at each
Two more tears appear,
To make up
The awesome necklace.
She looks and weeps—
Mary, the humble wife,
Who baked, swept, made beds,
And saw the glory of God
Her Son;
Who never knew
Where the next coin
Would come from
To buy the corn
To make the flat, delicious bread
Of Israel
To feed the man
Who was God,
And Who had created all the corn
And all that went into the coin of the realm!
Mary, the Mother of Jesus of Nazareth,
Whose Son
For thirty years,
Lived in a little village
Without pomp or glory
And Who cursed the Pharisees
As only God can curse.

She stands there, in the chapel,
The Mother of Meekness Incarnated.
And all the virtues could be seen
Through eyes that could see.

While they
Compromise,
Decide,
Deride, and work
Against the red
They wear!

Fools!
Don't they understand
That the red
Is the blood of Her Son?
The necklace is a visible sight
Of Mary's second sorrow.

Who wants to touch this necklace?
Angels tremble
Because they have to pick it up
And place it
In His hands;
And He,
With a face set,
Puts it away
Until the day
When one will stand
Before Him,
Naked and dead.
Then two tears
Will be put
On the scales
Against him,
Tears that can be seen!

Fools! Go on your knees
In sackcloth and ashes.
With bare feet
Make amends;
Make your dioceses
The fertile soil for all.
Walk without compromise.
Quo Vadis?
Don't turn from His words.
Fools!
O you Cardinals, Archbishops, Bishops,
Beware!
For what chance
Have you
Against the tears
Of the Mother of God?

The Man in White
Gets up.
The chapel
Is just a chapel.
The statue isn't there.
As silently as She came
She disappears,
To the heavens
Where She abides.

Two angels
Picked the necklace up
And brought it to Her Son;
He knows what the Second Sorrow
Of His Mother
Looks like.

Amen.

The Third Sorrow

In greys that match the greys
Of clouds on rainy days,
In greys that shimmer like tears
That hang on the eyes and eyelids
Of sorrowful men and women,
In greys of autumn landscapes
Stilled by rains,
Our Lady moves.

There is a grey pallor
To Her face
That seems almost corpse-like—
As if She,
The Deathless Mother ·
Of the Uncreated God,
Experienced the presence of decay and rot.
There is about Her a strange tenseness
That is seldom observed
In Her
Who is the essence
Of tranquility and peace.

She comes from heaven
Unobserved,
Her greys melting
With clouds of grey
That bring rain on earth.
Her dress is grey.
So is the cape.
So is the veil.
So seems the face.

O Lady
Dressed in grey,
What are you seeking?
She stands strangely lost
In some forlorn corner
Of the earth
That rain has drenched
And left as desolate
As earth can be.

Late in fall
When winter has not come
To hide all
'Neath its shroud of white.
She seems forlorn too.
Her feet are without shoes.
Bare.
They are the only thing
Alive in Her.
They move
While standing still—
As if She were making ready
To kill something
Coming through the grass.

There is a watchfulness in Her
That frightens us;
There is a power too
That seems to grow.
And sorrow lies within the heart
Of this strange power that grows.

The stillness of the air
Is rent with sounds
That screech

In torment.
Now She seems to collect Herself.
She is more powerful,
More sorrowful,
More watchful.

The sounds grow more strident,
Piercing,
Unharmonious.
They seem to come
From some hellish mind—
An orchestra
Composed of instruments
That contradict each other,
That fight each other to the death
With sounds—
If you can grasp the idea.
A waltz macabre from Spain.
Jazz jumps and kills a light refrain.
Symphony suddenly is cacophony.
A song that dies on a wrong harsh note.

The greys are greyer now.
They seem to move.
And the more they move
The more they look
Like Death
And then one understands.
Those were not sounds.
THEY WERE ACTS OF DISOBEDIENCE
The world over.
Disobedience is disharmony
Led by pride
And conducted by
The prince of pride.
Look how the puppets dance—
Children, men, women!!

Where are those
Who are obedient?
It seems that
The whole world
Is in that strange
Immense dance-hall.

Our Lady shivers.
This is what crucified Her Son.
The cross was of disobedience and pride.
On it hung
He Who was
Humility,
And was obedient
Unto death.
Her third unknown sorrow
Is to look
At Her own children
And see them breaking,
All night and day,
The bones of Her beloved.

It is like that.
It claws and tears you
And breaks your bones,
Puts them together
And starts all over.
Christ is not only crucified by it
But is torn to pieces;
His Kingdom stopped
And Satan growing.

What a dance hall!
What a stench!
What disharmony!
And behold

The Mother of all Beauty
Is lying, as if
Dying,
On dead grass.
And clouds of grey
Are covering Her
So full of grace,
As if they wanted to console Her,
But they weep;
And rain falls on the earth.

The foot that once
Crushed the head of the devil
Is motionless as if dead,
For the free will of Her children
Can resurrect the devil
Every time.

She lies there
Beneath grey skies
And cries
And cries
So much
Over
Her third unknown sorrow!

The Fourth Sorrow

Red like the blood of Christ
And strangely uneven—
The red, I mean—
In Her robe and cloak;
Changing with light
As if it were alive
And dripping, dripping blood
As She moved, knelt, and got up again.
It seems She stands
In a strange forest
No one knows
How did She come to be there?
From heaven She slipped, unnoticed,
Into this strangely dead place.

The trees are trees;
And yet they are not,
For they have turned to stone
As if unable to continue their growth
From the cursed earth.
There are mountains in the distance
That are fantastic in shape.
The landscape is surrealistic, and dark
Against the drop curtains of the sky.
And yet, there is some sort of illumination
That does not come
From moon or sun or stars.
It is as if some hidden floodlights
Were directed from below
Upon Her

Who stands dripping blood—
Or is it just the shimmer
Of Her clothing?

The air is still,
As if expecting a storm;
And heavy,
As air is wont to be
At times like this.
And heavy is the unbound hair
Of the Virgin.
It seems to pull Her head
Quite back.
Her eyes are open, staring,
With something akin to horror
If that can be;
For the Mother of God and men
Is seldom horrified.

She has seen all there is to be seen
Of pain and sorrow.
And yet that is the way
She looks to me.

Quite unexpectedly
The drop curtains are parted,
And against the surrealistic landscape
Of the hills,
A hundred million homes are opened.
And eyes can encompass
Every one of them.

A home should be
The indwelling place of love,
But it is not always so.
Here a man and a woman

Can be seen in the deep, intimate
Embrace of love,
And yet—Oh blasphemy!
Oh travesty of God!—
They act like beasts,
For they prevent the birth of a soul
Allotted to their love!
The tree of it is sterile,
Fruit-less,
Like the cursed fig tree of old.
No wonder then
That all the trees
Around Her
Are of stone.
That is how they got there,
From homes that refused birth
Came this forest of stone!

There and there and there—
Thousands, millions,
That same sight.
The forest of stone trees
Is growing denser
And crying for vengeance
As only stones
Can cry to heaven.
And She
That is dripping drops of blood—
Or is it just the folds
Of cloak and dress—
Seemingly unable
To bear the stress
Of such a sight,
Falls down
On Her knees
And lifts up Her cloak.

O Mary, the Immaculata!
All covered with His blood,
She stands
Against the trees of stone
Herself transfigured
In the horror of it,
A Woman
Colored in the color of it—
For horror too is red.

But what is this?
It seems as if
The cloak has fallen
With Her arms—
(As if they were dead).
She is not kneeling any more.
One outstretched hand
Is on a stone.
The raven black hair
Is scattered
All over it,
And contrasts with
Her cloak of red.
She is moaning
As if there were no room
For tears.
Fleet of foot,
She dashes
From one home
To another,
Where men and women
Are ready
To murder
Their offspring.

The gentle hands of Mary,
God's Mother,
Pick up
Each mutilated little corpse
Abortion brought.
She unbuttons the red cloak.
Its lining is white
Like Her virginal soul.
She takes the little bodies
And gently buries them
In a nice field;
And as She does,
The daisies
And other field flowers
Decorate and cover
The endless little graves.
But oh! the souls
Of the little corpses
She takes into Her mantle
Lined with white,
And, like a Mother,
Holds them tight.

Abortion! Birth control!
What parents do to children
That came in spite of all
They did to prevent their coming!
That strange, obscene
And hidden corner
Of a nation's soul
Which is a cancer
Growing, growing—
Which is the foundation
Of today's malady of mind.
That is Mary's fourth unknown sorrow—
And indeed it is most great

Because it is so widespread
And something must be done
To stop it.
The Three-in-One
Will take much from man.
One created,
One redeemed,
One overshadowed them.
One is three,
And Three is One.
He who touches Mary
Deals with Her Father,
Her Son,
And Her Most Holy Spouse,
The Crimson Dove!

And if a sorrow
Penetrates too deeply
Into the heart
Of the Immaculata,
Then the Three
Will rise in anger.
And the Sodoms and Gomorrahs
Of today
Will cease to be!
Amen.

The Fifth Sorrow

Purple! Not the purple of violets,
   Nor then again of irises—
Tall, slender, growing in the Spring
And waving with light purple wings
At all the winds.
A purple dark! Of mourning and pain.
A purple of Lent, hushed silences,
And shed and unshed tears.
A heavy purple
That seems to weigh
The slender figure down
From toe to crown.
She moves
With a strange slowness,
As if quite unable
To bear the weight
Of all this purple,
That rustles
As She walks
With little rustling whispers
That hold within themselves
The echo of tragic sounds.

The rim of heaven is reached,
With pain,
With infinite slowness.
She lifts Her hands
And makes wings of the purple stuff,
And plummets earthward
With terrific speed.

The purple stuff
Is heavy
And weighs Her down.
She falls upon the earth
And cries out in pain.
She lies on a road—
A purple stain
That blends somehow
With the grey dust of the road,
A lonely road
That by-passes
All big ones.
Abruptly She seems to vanish.
You see Her again
In a big city
With towering buildings
That pierce the sky—
In the midst of throngs
That hurry by.

Her purple
Blends with the dirty grey
Of buildings large and small,
And makes Her inconspicuous
To all.
Quietly She enters a church.
The front pews here are
Occupied by an elegant crowd,
On display—hats and such—
Conspicuous.
Our Lady is grieved
Beyond grieving.
Their hearts are cold and poor,
Yet they come,
Dressed up,
On a Sunday,
To Mass.

As She watches the priest
Lift up the host,
She remembers a day, a hill.
The purple is stained
By Her tears.
How proper and correct
The people are,
And ostentatious
To the collection plate!
But how could their hearts!
"Pharisees," She cries.
Unable to stay
As Her Son
Dies a mystical death upon the altar.

Again
The purple is stained
With tears.
Again She slips away
Like a tired woman
In a shroud.

Again the city streets,
Again a door.
A flat or an apartment,
Rooms well furnished,
Carpets soft,
And people talking
About a forthcoming marriage.

There's a priest,
Young and eager and clean,
But his voice
Seems to bounce
From his hearers' hearts
Like peas from a wall.

He speaks the words of Her Son.
Mary smiles,
And places Her hand
Upon his head.

But they are adamant.
"What does it matter
If our daughter
Marries
Outside the Church?
He is rich,
And it is obsolete
To wear your religion
On your sleeve."
Our Lady collapses
At the foot
Of the priests.
She is listening to a story
"There was a king
Who had a big feast
And sent out messengers
To invite;
But one was busy, selling,
One had taken a wife…"

Without tears
She leaves the place
And takes the priest
With Her.
The door slams
As if someone
Had nailed a coffin lid.

At twilight
You might see
A woman
Dressed in purple

Kneel in a city church
Somewhere,
Merging with the shadows,
Her tears dropping
One by one.
The modern Pharisees,
And those who mock Her Son
By calling themselves
Lying names,
And those
Who answer rudely
When He calls them to a feast—
These are the fifth sorrow of Mary.

And what breaks one's heart
Is that
She weeps
And weeps.

Come!
Let us console Her
If we may.

The Sixth Sorrow

There is no color at all today
  Not even grey.
Maybe there are some browns—
Dirty,
Verging on black,
Here and there.

It is not to be seen,
Is colorless, or is
An everyday sort of color
That passes unnoticed.
The poor sometimes wear it
In cheap, washed, second-hand clothing—
Indefinite,
Indescribable.

It is pitiful
To see
The Queen of heaven
Thus arrayed.
It suits Her ill, somehow.
Her attire has no shape.
Its washed-out blue-greys
Have a transparency
That makes one sick.
She seems to shiver in Her clothes.
Are they too big?
They don't seem to fit anywhere,
And She wears them
With a pain

That makes one wish
To clothe Her
With the robes
Of gold and silver
Brocade
That are so fitting for Her,
The Queen of all things
Seen and unseen.

She goes
On errands
That seem diffuse,
And washed-out,
Like the clothes
She wears.
What a strange sight!
My God!
The pain of it!

What are you seeking,
Beggar Maid?
You move so swiftly
Through our earth
Its hamlets, villages, and towns!
You cover
 In a space of seconds
One half the world.

What are you seeking,
Beggar Maid?
She keeps
Searching, looking,
Hastening on,
Stopping here and there
An instant,
Then with a wringing of hands,
Goes on again.

What are you looking for,
Beggar Maid?
She goes
Into a church
And swiftly comes out,
Her hands
Expressing pain
And doubt.
She enters that college, this school,
That belongs to Her Son,
And leaves
In haste even greater.

The pain in Her hands
Becomes almost a chant;
And their movement is slower.
It seems as if
With a supplicatory gesture,
They transfer their agony
Into Her heart.
You can see
Seven swords
Coming from it,
Their strangely-wrought handles resting
Upon the wishy-washy fabric
Of her second-hand clothes.

Now, half-sitting
Half-kneeling,
She rests
Against a tree trunk
On some forgotten road;
And we—
By some force compelled—
(We do not know
From whence, nor how)

We must retrace
Her steps
And know
What it is
The Beggar Maid
In second-hand clothes
Was seeking
And did not find;
And why
She weeps by the tree trunk.

We have not Her speed.
It takes us endless time,
It seems,
To walk
With our human feet
Where Hers
Were so fast and fleet.

But we get there.
And when
The strange pilgrimage
Is done,
We too are weary,
And wring our hands
With all the pain
That is in us!

For even we,
So human
And so small,
Begin to understand.
The Queen of heaven
Covered the earth
In search
OF GREATNESS IN HUMAN SOULS;

And wept because
She did not find it.
For true greatness is
Humility, and hiddenness,
And nothingness,
Whose only claim to greatness
Is being in love
With Love
Who is Her Son;
And totally surrendered
To His Will
As She is.

She made the round of earth
And what did She find?
Mediocrity.
She did not mind
Hate or coldness.
But mediocrity
Among the children
Of His blood
She could not stand.

Perhaps She started out
From Heaven,
Dressed in Her queenly robes.
But they,
Coming on contact
With mediocrity,
Would become
Wishy-washy,
And change
Into greys and blues
Of indiscriminate hues.

She is still there
When we come back;
Still sitting
By a big tree-trunk
On that forgotten road;
Her hands
Against Her face,
Our Lady of La Salette
In second-hand clothes
That reflect our mediocrity.
To assuage the
"Sitio"
Of Her Son.
How could She
Go back to heaven,
She who is forever seeking
Souls in love.

That is the sixth unknown sorrow
Of Our Lady—
By the tree trunk
On a forgotten road.

(Let you and me
Go to Her, now,
And fill Her heart;
So that She can give
A drink
To Her Son.)

Amen.

The Seventh Sorrow

Green, the color of hope!
Bedecked in it,
She seems
To hug it close
To Her eternally Virgin breast,
As if that hope
Was desperate
Against all hope.

It is not just a green
Of this shade or that.
It contains
Within itself
All the shades;
The light,
The dark,
The in-betweens,
Creating
As She walks
The illusion of Spring.
Oh friend, who passes by,
It is Illusion that you see.
When She comes
Against that light
The green seems strangely dead,
As green leaves die
From the frostbites of late fall, and
Change into the dirty brown
Of leaves
That strew

A frozen ground.
And still
She holds Her cape
Of light and tender green,
That gives illusion
Of the Spring,
Tight
Against Her breast,
As if She hopes
Against all hope.

What are the currents,
Or whence the winds,
That waft
Or bring Her down
On their streams
As gently
As the leaf
Is lifted up
And then laid down
By a gay spring breeze?
There is nothing
Of the spring
In the wind
That brings Her down
From the glorious heavens.
It is a sort of a dead wind
That serves Her simply
As a road
From there to earth.
And there She stands—
Slight, beautiful,
In gentle hues of green
That She hugs to Her breast
As if She hopes
Against all hope.

And now swiftly,
And now hesitantly,
And now slowly,
She wends Her way
Hither, thither, yon.
And who can say
What is Her goal?
If you look close
You may understand
What our Lady
Dressed in green
Is looking for;
And also you may guess
Where she goes.

It is quite simple
If you look close.

She goes into the hearts of men.
She looks for just one heart
That is filled
With the desire
For the Desired One—
Her Son.
But what does
Our Lady
Dressed in green,
Who clutches Her cape
As one who clutches hope
Against all hope,
Find in the hearts of men?

She finds an endless swirl;
Movement and chaos
That for a moment becomes order.
(But what disorder in that order!)
Out of that chaos

Are shaped
All kinds of idols,
That stand still
For a moment
And then fall back into the chaos
Of desires!
But where is the desire for Him
Who is the
Desire of the eternal hills?

Behold those hearts
All bound.
All attached to self.
A turgid stream
That hasn't strength enough
To become
A torrent,
Or to dance,
Gayly,
Madly,
Over some stones
Warmed
By the sun of love!
A turgid
Stream of self
That flows
In a sort of
Mushy, sprawled-out way—
So that
You can't say
Whence it comes
Nor where it goes.
One could surmise
That from self
It starts,
And to self
It goes.

And none would stay,
Over long,
In such a heart
For the dead, dark, putrid
Stream of self
Gives off too great a stench!

But Our Lady
Is not like that.
She enters
Such a heart;
And like
The woman in the Gospel
Who lost the groat,
She searches
All through
The turgid stream
To see
If She can find
One tiny penny
Of true desire
For Her Son.

If so, then She would
Spring-clean
That heart;
Open its windows,
Let the sun and air
Come in;
And then sit down in it—
The Lady in Hope Green!
And just by being there,
She would bring Spring,
Young and green,
Into that heart,
That would awaken

The desire
For Her Son—
Who is the
Lover of the soul
And comes
When turtle doves are heard
And Spring comes to the land
To seek His love.

Yes, Our Lady
Seeks in turgid, stinking
Streams of self
A penny's worth of the desire
Of Her Son—

And does not find it!
She leaves the heart
Alone—
To self.
She wanders from heart to heart.
Vainly She seeks the
Desire of Her Son.

Look at the changes
In Her dress and cape.
When She started
She wore the tender greens of Spring.
And darker hues,
And all tones in-between.
And now Her dress is stained.
Her face has streaks of dirt.
Her hands smell of the odor
Of all the souls
She entered.
She departs
Without having found
In any of the

Millions of selfish hearts
A true desire
For Her Son.
Her dress turns brown,
The color of dead leaves.
She sits and weeps,
As she wept yesterday,
Her posture still the same.

Our Lady of La Salette—
Without La Salette,
Without a crown—
In dirty brown!
This is the seventh unknown sorrow
Of the Queen of Heaven.

The Seven Unknown Glories of Mary

The First Glory

Gold and silver, mixed together
Strand by strand,
Not woven by human hands,
Bedeck Her slender form.
She walks,
A Queen of two realms—
(Of which She is the bridge)
Heaven and earth.

He made Her thus,
Because He is the Way.
And the Way
Needs a bridge
To cross
From Infinity to finity.
She is that bridge
The Woman
Clad in gold and silver cloth
Not made on earth
Nor woven by human hand.

The humble Maid of Nazareth
Stands here, bedecked
In rubies, emeralds,
Pearls, and diamonds
That are like stars
And make around Her,
From head to toes,
A shimmering, dancing,
Twinkling background

That would dazzle men's eyes
If they could see.

She stands,
A light Herself,
Reflecting
A greater Light
That seems to pass
Through Her
Effulgence bright!
But what is this?
The Queen in all Her glory
Bends low
And gathers up
From the earth
Some strange and simple things.

I can not see
What it looks like.
From far away
It seems like a handful
Of pebbles grey.
And, strange as this may seem,
She takes them out of human souls!
How swift and eager
Her movements!
With each grey pebble
Her face becomes more radiant.
It resembles
The rising sun
Somehow.

And now,
Not content
To have Her hands
Full of such seemingly useless things,
She lifts

Her heavy cloak of gold
(Or is it Her cape?)
And makes a basket
Of it.

She gathers more pebbles
Snatching them up
Recklessly,
Like a child at play,
But are they pebbles?
I can not see.
She is too swift
For eyes like mine.
She stands erect, majestic, gay,
With the cloak of gold—
(Or is it Her cape?)
Clutched tight
In Her hands—
A basket resplendent!

Up
She goes,
An eager flame of gold,
A candle of the Lord
Burning bright.

And now She is there.
She runs and trips
And runs again
Over heavenly floors,
Which, of course,
For Her,
Are angel's wings
Eagerly outspread.
She runs and lays
The little grey pebbles
Into His lap

And, laughs,
And, laughs,
The laughter gay
Of a Queen
Who is still
A Girl of fifteen,
And has just brought
Her Son
A toy or two
To play with
In the meadows green.

He smiles
Into Her upturned face,
And picks,
With kingly grace,
The pebbles up.
Lo! What is this?
At His touch
They become
A crown
Of beauty!
Diamonds, emeralds, and rubies
Pale into insignificance
Before the glorious sheen
The small gay pebbles
Have been given!

She stands
Before Him
With folded hands,
Expectant,
And now the hands
Unfold themselves,
And strip Her robes
Of all their heavenly jewels.
Gently She lays these

At His feet.
She kneels.
Inclines Her head;
And heaven is still.

A ray of light
Comes down
Upon Her.
It must be
God the Father
Smiling on Her;
And then there is
A swish of wings
And some crimson tinges
Fall lovingly
On the bent head.
Her spouse,
The Holy Ghost,
Is there.
Her Son
Picks up the crown
And kisses it
And puts it
On Her head,
And now I know
The first strange unknown glory
Of Our Lady.

She went
And gathered Herself
A crown
From the hidden and humble souls
That loved Her Son
In the simplicity
Of the pure of heart.

The strangest thing about it
Is that She found them
Not where men look for them.
(True humility and simplicity
It seems,
Are found where worldly men
Are not!)

The crown shines
Resplendent.
But you and I
Can add to it.
Each little hidden
Grey pebble of us
Can make another Glory
For the Mother of God;
And provide another drop of love
For the eager lips
Of Her Son.
Amen. Amen.

The Second Glory

Scarlet!
A strange red.
The color of flames
That just begin
To kiss the wood.
And then again
The color of fire
That destroys and sears
And burns and eats up
All domains.
And yet again
The scarlet of the poppies
That grow in such profusion
In Palestine;
That used to run
And nestle
Against the seamless robes
Of Her Son;
That loved
To be crushed to death
By His holy feet
And lay there bleeding
After He passed,
Dying
For love of Him.

Such is the scarlet
Of Her robe today.
Her mantle is of purest white,
That catches here and there,
The flames of Her scarlet robe.

She is very sure tonight.
Her movements
Are neither slow nor fast.
Purposeful and strong,
She descends;
Walking on air
As we do
On the ground.
She knows
Where She is going
Tonight.
You won't believe it—
But I see it.
She walks
On the great white ways of sin—
The Sinless One!

Without hesitation
She enters
Cocktail lounges,
Cafes,
Cabarets,
Dives on the waterfront, and
Burlesque show houses.
Up and down
The world's most sinful ways,
The Sinless walks.
Each time
She stops,
Inside or outside,
The flaming scarlet
Of Her robe
Leaps up—
A living fire—
And touches
The heart

Of some Magdalen,
Some forgotten one
Who fell
Into the black, broad ways
Of man's inhumanity
To man.

A strange cortege
Is formed.
The Woman
In the scarlet robe and the
White cape,
The burning flame of love,
The Mother of God,
Walks on ahead
Through all the sinful ways
Of men's cities,
Towns, and villages.
And right behind Her,
One by one,
Are women and men
Who were touched
By the leaping, living flames
Of Her scarlet robe;
And who,
In the twinkling
Of an eye,
Turned
From a life of sin
To a life of love,
Bathed in tears
Of sorrow and pain.

Incredible
The sight!
Incredible, but true!
There She is,

All scarlet;
Sure, queenly, and straight.
And there they are!
How long is now the line
That walks behind Her!
It grows and grows.
It turns into a multitude—
Into hosts of souls!

But suddenly
The long procession
Disappears!
The lady in the scarlet robes
Is capeless
Her black hair
Is streaming down.
It covers up
The back
Of Her red robe.
But in Her hands
She holds the cape,
White and immaculate.
And now one hears
A mighty swishing of wings.
And Seraphim
(Or are they Cherubim?)
Are holding the cape
Four-corner wise.
Behold Our Lady
Lifting high the heart of each
Of the sinful ones
That left
The ways of sin
For the ways of love
Because She came
Into the cocktail lounges,
The cafes,

The cabarets,
The dives,
The burlesque shows.

She takes
The repentant hearts,
All aquiver with love,
And places them,
One by one
Into Her seamless robe
Held by the angels
(Are they Cherubim or Seraphim?
I cannot tell.
But they are mighty,
That I know.)

And now,
Up She goes;
And they behind,
Holding the hearts
Of sinners
Who turned
From sin
To love;
And love, of course,
You know, is God,
And God is
The Son of Her
Who now mounts back
A flame—
My lady of the scarlet robe!

And at the feet
Of the Three-in-One,
She lays
Her stainless cape
Filled with hearts

Of sinful men and women
Who left
The ways of sin
For those of love.
Heaven is filled
With such a gladness
That I cannot see.
Who can look
At the joy of heaven
Over one repentant heart?
But here there are thousands!

God the Father,
Unseen yet felt—
A ray of light—
Touches the hearts
And they become
One beating heart,
The Son bends down
And lifts it up
And hands it
To the Holy Spirit,
The Crimson Dove,
Our Lady's Spouse.

From that one heart
A thousand flames
Shoot up.
The Spouse bends low,
With love aglow,
And hands the pulsating, loving heart
Of repentant sinners—
Thousands in one—
To His beloved Mary.
And She,
Delighted, overjoyed
At the joy

Of the Uncreated Three,
To the psalmody
Of all in heaven,
Places their heart
Into Her own!

And lo!
They blend,
The fire of love,
The Mother's heart
And that
Of the returned prodigals.

There is the
Second unknown glory
Of our Lady
In heaven.

The Third Glory

White,
    A strange white.
Dazzling, but
Not the white of snow.
Nor the white
Of any earth fabric
Of clouds
Against the blue sky
Not the white of flour.
No—a heavenly white
All aglow
From within.
The white of light
Not seen on earth.
That is Her dress today.

Her cape is yellow
The yellow of crushed wheat,
The kind that is ground
Reverently, slowly,
By hand,
And that is made into bread—
Altar bread—
To go with the wine
That together form
The Body and Blood
Of Her Son,
Christ our Lord.
Yes, the cape is yellow—
The yellow

Of fresh-ground wheat flour,
Tender and light,
Blending perfectly
With the heavenly white.

Slowly descending,
Holding the yellow cape
Close to Her breast
With Her head
Bent down a little,
Her eyes downcast
And the black eyelashes
Throwing a shadow
On Her beautiful face,
Our Lady comes,
With unspeakable grace,
In a strange, recollected silence
Of peace.

Light as thistledown
She touches the earth,
And treads
Its fields and streams,
Its roads and lanes.
Never lifting Her eyes,
She seems to know
Where She has to go.
There is in Her
A glow
That seems to make
All it touches
Feel Her joy
As She passes by!

Nature itself
Sings the divine office
In praise of Her.

Rivers and streams,
And the ocean, it seems,
Chant Matins and Lauds
As She passes by.
The trees,
As they see Her,
Chant Prime.
Grass and flowers
Sing the little hours.
Hedges and bushes
Come in with Vespers,
And birds and insects
Flutter with joy
As they sing Compline.
They fly and fly
In a halo
Around Her head while
Little glow-worms
Light Her way.
A beautiful sight
To behold, indeed—
Our Lady
In heavenly white,
Still, recollected,
Smiling,
As She passes by
And listens to nature
Sing to Her
The divine praises
Of God,
Her Father,
Son
And Spouse.

But where is She going?
She started
When Matins began.

Now Compline
Is being sung
And all are at rest.
Where
Can She be going
In the middle of the night?
The moon
Does not ask
Any questions,
It just lights the way,
And kisses
The hem
Of Her yellow cape,
Turning it
Into a strange, enchanting
Lamé
The stars just follow Her,
Wherever She goes,
And glow,
And glow,
To show
That they are delighted
By what they see
And can not contain
Their glee.

She has stopped
At a church.
One old and small.
Not grand at all.
And the presbytery
Is unpainted.
Unprepossessing, grey
And mercilessly beaten
By time and rains.
Our Lady knocks
(Very gently and reverently)

At the sagging door.
It opens.
And there is an old priest smiling there—
As shabby
As the rectory.

The Queen of heaven
Curtsies low,
And says,
"O Father
May I pray come in?"
The wrinkled face
Lights up
With joy,
And the clear blue eyes
Of a child
Fill with tears
At so much grace.
He falls on his knees
And tries to kiss
The hem
Of Her heavenly white robe
Or yellow cape.
But no!
She will not let him,
She holds him up,
And (can you imagine?)
She kneels before him
Humble and still.

With trembling hands,
The old priest
Makes over Her
The sign
Of Her Son,
And pronounces words
So full of life

In a tongue
Dead
More than a thousand years.
Our Lady,
Still kneeling—
A white candle,
Burning
With light,
Catches
The blessing
In Her cupped hands;
And,
Kissing the hand
That gave it to Her,
Vanishes
As if She had not been there.

From rectory
To rectory,
From monastery
To monastery,
She goes.
Is She
On a pilgrimage?
Perhaps.
Our Lady
Tonight
Collects
The blessing
Of holy priests.

Oh, look at that!
Again She has taken
The yellow cape off
And She holds it tight,
For there within
Its golden glow

Lie the precious stones
That were
But a minute ago
The blessings of holy priests
On Her bent head.
And now suddenly
She is lifted up
And is back in heaven again.

God, the Father,
Bends from the throne
As our Lady,
Dressed in heavenly white
Lifts the yellow cape high.
There is a light from the Unseen One.
And a voice is heard
That is rarely heard
Even in heaven.
"I am well pleased,
For these are the blessings
Of My very own Son!"

At the words,
The blessings
Become stars
And fall
On the heavenly white
Of Mary's gown,
To reveal
The third unknown glory
Of the Queen of Stars in Heaven.

The Fourth Glory

Grey.
But not like the grey
She wore before.
A tender grey.
Quite inconspicuous.
The grey that goes
Into the simple rough dress
Of the religious
Of La Sagesse.
The cape—white.
A working-woman's white.
As aprons in a convent
Are white.
Or coifs.
Yet not the prim, proper
Coifs of choir nuns.
No! the soft and simple apparel
Of working sisters.
Her feet are encased
In wooden shoes—
The kind
That hired girls wear
While doing chores.
Or poor nuns use
In some far distant places
Of our earth.
Our Lady
Descends from heaven today
A working woman;
Or a poor nun.
I cannot say which.

Or maybe she is
A slave of olden days.
Her mien
Is humble,
Effacing,
As She walks.
Her grey
Blends well
With sidewalks
And rural roads
That both are clad
In various shades of it.
Humble, unobtrusive,
She glides
Through crowds
Or walks quietly
Along the sides of roads.
She is the same
Lady of heaven
They sing about—
"Regina coeli."
And yet
No one would know that
Who passed by
So quietly is She dressed
In Her warm grey.

Today She is not alone.
Behind Her
Walks a man
A priest—
His face enraptured.
He does not see a thing
Except
Our Lady

Dressed in warm grey.
Right behind him,
A few paces,
There is another—
A woman.
She too
Is dressed in grey,
As dairy-maids
And servants
Used to be
In the seventeenth century
In France.
Her feet are shod
In wooden shoes.
They make much more noise
Than those
The Queen of heaven
Wears.

Why, look, see!
That is Saint Louis de Montfort;
And the girl
Who founded
Les Filles de Sagesse.
That is most strange.
Where are the three
Going at this stage?
Our Lady
Seems to be utterly unaware
These two
Are following Her;
And She stops
At the most strange places;
Now up the steps
Of palaces
Fit for kings;
Into bed chambers

Ornate and rich.
And now you see Her
At a dance,
With lights, music,
And romance.

Then suddenly the three,
(For Louis
And the other
Are right there
With Her)
Go to a hovel,
And, before you realize it,
To a hospital;
And then, quite unafraid,
To no-man's land
Where men die, or lie wounded.

It is a little hard
To follow.
Our Lady walks slowly—
And yet, in seconds,
She is in Shantung, Paris,
London, New York, Berlin,
Spain, Portugal, Africa,
Switzerland, Belgium,
Or Australia.
The Northland sees Her.
The Southland meets Her.
Canada, South America,
Why, the world!
She even slips in
Behind the Iron Curtain!

All countries
See Her today
As She walks

Demurely
Dressed in grey.
All I can see
Is that
She stops
And seems to talk
In all those places
To this one or that
As they dance
Or work
Or pass Her by.

There is no rhyme or reason
That I can see
Why She should talk
To them all.
They come from
All states of life,
Nuns, priests,
Lay people,
Young and old,
Single and married.
Extraordinary sight indeed!
You can find
Even children
In their midst.

And now it is eventide,
And She is standing
On the beach
An utterly forlorn lonely shore
Where weary ocean waves
Beat gently at Her feet.
Well!
She has left
Her wooden shoes
On the sandy beach,

And slowly She ascends—
Her grey blending
With the twilight
That swiftly seems to change
Into the eventide
And there is Louis de Montfort
And the nun in grey
Still behind Her
And after them
Follow men and women
Enough to make a solid line
'Twix earth and Heaven!

They number thousands
And they all go up.

Why! They were the people
That Our Lady talked to
Tonight.
They don't look
Quite like they did
A little while ago;
There is a strange new glow
About them,
And a transparency
That was not apparent then
But is now.

There they are—
All up in heaven—
All the thousands
Of them.
And they advance
In a strange formation.
Our Lady goes ahead.
Her greys have changed.
They have the translucency

Of a diamond,
And the grey
Within it
Has turned
To shooting rays of blue
Like the most precious diamonds do.
Behind Her
The two
That went everywhere
With Her—
The priest
And the nun—
Shine too
With a lesser light,
As if they had
A halo bright
From head to toe.
And in a semicircle wide,
In serried ranks,
The rest stand
Before the throne of God.

If you look on this
From above
It appears to be
The formation
Of a diadem,
And so it is!
Because the Holy Spirit,
The Crimson Dove,
The God of Love,
Lifts up the lot—
Leaving His Spouse
Standing below
He places
The priest
And the nun

In the front
Of the diadem,
And those in the serried ranks
Wherever He wants them.
And they form a crown
Of precious stones
And gold!

Lovingly
The Holy Spirit
Places the crown
On the Jewel of heaven,
Mary,
The Mother of God!

Could you guess
Who the rest
Of the people were?
Why! Slaves of Mary!
They form the crown
Of gold and precious stones
For the Queen of heaven!

They are Her fourth unknown glory
In heaven.

The Fifth Glory

Red.
Red again.
The brilliant red of blood
Gushing forth
From a thousand wounds;
Unrelieved by anything.
Just red
Is the gown,
And so the cape.
Our Lady is dressed
In pure red today
Nothing but red.

The robe is long
With a strange train
She didn't have before.
It seems to be,
As She descends,
A rivulet of blood.
Behind Her feet
The sky
Reflects the red
As She passes by.
So does the earth.
All things
That come within
Its ken
Turn red.

Her face is strange
It is exultant
And yet underneath
There is the reflection
Of God's justice.
She descends from heaven
In all Her majesty;
And angels follow Her
With reverence.
Their wings reflect
The red of the gown
From underneath,
And in their hands
They hold
Enormous chalices
Of gold.

Our Lady
Passes by
Most of earth,
But enters, purposefully,
One part of it
Divided
From the rest
By an unseen wall
Of steel.
She makes Her way
Through a strange terrain
Of rolling rivers
Of muddy brown.
She enters
Strange looking towns
Made of flimsy bamboo houses.
She is in China.

She stops
In many places.

At Her touch,
Doors that are locked
And padlocked
With many locks
Open easily.
She doesn't stop
In prisons
Dank and dark;
She makes Her way
Into their courtyards.

A gory sight
Meets Her eye.
But she is
Calm, collected,
Yet exultant.
She comes
At a time
Of execution
(Or is it just a slaughter?)
Or then again
Perhaps it is not China
At all;
But Palestine—
The hill of Calvary
Three crosses
On one of which
Hangs Her Son?

Into the courtyard
Is dragged
A man in black.
He has some red
About him
About the throat.
The red
Matches Her robe.

It is blood red.
No! It is in
His skull cap.

I cannot see clearly.
There are too many
In front of me;
All soldiers,
They push and scream.
They tie him
To the trunk
Of a small tree.
They spit on him.
They speak, sing-song wise,
Strange words
That sting.
Then, obedient to a shout,
They attack and bayonet him
As if he were
A sack
That soldiers practise on!

Before he died,
He saw the Lady
In robes of red—
Blood red—
And his face
Knew Her!
The Queen of Martyrs!
He did not feel
The bayonets.
He saw Her smile
Just as he died.
And the red blood
Of him
Flew out
Of a thousand wounds.

Two angels
Gathered it up,
His blood,
Into a chalice
Finely wrought.

Our Lady
Watched the soul
Go up, and up
Into the sky—
An arrow straight
To God
On high.
And She went on—
From execution
To execution
From China to Burma,
Indo-China;
Into the rear
Of the huge mountains
Of India,
And from there
Into Russia.

Everywhere She went
The angels followed.
There was a host of them.
Each pair
Held an immense chalice.
Most of them
Were filled
With the blood of martyrs.

One chalice waited
To be filled.
Our Lady,

Swiftly now,
Went through the mountains
Far in the north,
Where trees grow short,
And days
Have no nights
To rest in.
And there,
On an island
Most holy,
Dedicated to her
Some eight hundred years ago—
Or so they say—
She stopped
Before a saw mill,
Where strange emaciated men
Worked
Like shadows on a screen.

She stopped
Before a tattered figure.
Unrecognizable were his clothes—
And yet red seemed uppermost
About them,
Though there was no red
In them,
At all.
I cannot tell why
But it seemed
As if red
Belonged to him—
The red of blood.

He was busy
At a strange task.
He was taking the bark
Off a tree

With his bare hands.
They were all broken up;
And blood colored the bank,
And seeped into the tree
Beneath the bark.
He must have been doing that
For the longest time!
His hands were
Just wounds—
Bleeding on all sides.
Trying to get the bark
Off the tree,
With hands
That were just pulp.

Our Lady
Dressed in red
Stood by
And watched.
The angels
With chalices
Watched too.
And one pair
Put the empty chalice,
At Her command,
Right under
The bleeding hands.

At this moment
A man well-clad
Appeared
With a whip.
He let the whip fall
On the man
With the mangled hands.
It cut straight through
His flimsy clothes

And left a trail of red
Upon his back.
The man lifted the whip again
And again drew blood.
The victim
Stumbled twice,
Fell down
On the stony ground,
And died!

Our Lady bent low
And took the soul
Of the dead man—
That was so white,
So full of glow—
And then looked up
Into heaven.
A bolt of lightning
Fell
And killed the man
With the whip.

A great fear came
Upon everyone.
But Our Lady did not linger
On the holy island.
She was already
Soaring upwards;
Behind Her,
Her train
Making a river of blood,
With the soul
Of the man
With the mangled hands.
There was about it
A radiance
That blinded one.

At the gates
Many shining souls
Met Her;
And all waved palms,
For all were martyrs
For the faith.
But the two
We spoke of,
The first and the last,
Were suddenly bedecked
In robes of bishops' red—
The robes that prelates wear
To show the world
That they are ready
To die
For God,
Even as these two had died.

You should see
How well their red
Blended
With the resplendent red
Of Mary's gown.
But then
Why shouldn't it?
She walked ahead again
And stood before the throne
Of the unseen and uncreated
Father—
Hers and our own.

And all the angels
With the martyrs' blood
In their chalices,
And all the souls
Of the martyrs,

Were below Her.
The Lord of Hosts
Received the chalices
And spilled them back
Onto the earth—
But not before
He blessed them.

The seed of martyrs
Is the seed of faith.
The souls of the two martyrs
He gave back to Mary
In a special way,
For martyrs form
Her fifth unknown glory
In heaven.
They are always
With Her
When She leaves the throne
And goes
Around about heaven
As She is wont to do,
A-visiting everyone,
As mothers like to do.

The Sixth Glory

The dress is gingham—
        Very up to date—
In simple lines.
The kind housewives wear
All day
Everywhere.
An apron over it.
Of any hue
That fits the dress.
The long black hair
Is neatly tied
Over the nape of the neck.
Nothing can be seen on the head.
Just hair.
Like every woman wears it
Today
But long, and
With a beautiful sheen
To it.
No ornaments of any kind.
Stockings and shoes
The same as every woman has today.
The shoes are low-healed
More like ballet slippers.

She comes down
From heaven,
Sure and demure;
As if She were
A modern housewife

Descending to start fires
Or make the family breakfast.
No angels around Her.
She is all alone.
And this time
She goes
From home to home.
No one pays the slightest notice
To the housewife
With blue-black hair
In a big knot
Over Her neck.
She seems to have
A shopping basket
That is finely made.

She enters home after home.
What does She see?
From some
She comes
Quite sad,
From others,
Quite glad.
It seems
That She prefers
The ones
Where there is
An awful lot
Of kids,
And things are not
Quite so tidy
As they should be
Because of it.
There She stays
A long time indeed.
And as She comes

Out of these houses,
Her basket bulges
(Or is it her bag?
Her shopping bag, I mean)
I do not know with what.

She by-passes certain homes.
And why?
They are pretty nice.
On the right street.
With lawns tidy and neat.
With shades drawn just so.
An air of comfort about them
And flowers in the proper place,
But somehow a little cold,
I grant.
No children.
Dogs, cats, cars.
No children; or
Just one or two—
Kind of droopy-looking inside,
If you know what I mean,
But quite smart outside.
She does not stop there.
Her face grows quite sad.
She averts her eyes
And hastens by.

The strangest thing of all—
She does not enter the front door;
She goes in the back way, or through
The kitchen.
(Our Lady of the Kitchen!
Or is it
Our Lady of the Broom?)

There are certain homes

Where She stays quite a time.
Probably giving a helping hand
With this and that.
When She comes out of homes
Like this
Her bag bulges
Wide, big.
I wonder
What is in it?

It is getting late.
Our Lady has been,
It seems,
Everywhere—
All over the place—
The United States,
Canada,
The rest of the world.
She has been in all homes.
And now Her strange basket
Or bag,
Is really bulging!

But She has covered it
With a red cloth,
And you can not see
What is in there.
I would like to peek
But I don't dare.
I cannot see
No matter which way
I look.
She does not look tired.
The basket is heavy,
But She carries it
With a great ease—
Though She isn't very tall.

I would like to help,
But there's no way I can,
Because She is going
Up to heaven
And I have to stay
Where I am.

Up She goes
In the twilight—
In Her ballet shoes
Ordinary housedress,
Neat apron,
And the rest.
And there She is
In front of Her Son.
Now we shall see
What is in the basket.

She smiles quite happily
As She lifts the red cloth.
And what do we see!
Why! Hearts!
A whole lot of them!
Beating merrily, happily.
They are strange hearts.
Two in one,
They beat in unison,
And around them
Is a crown of little hearts
That beat likewise
With the rhythm
Of the big ones.

Why that's simple!
Why didn't I guess?!
She brings to Christ
Little churches

Families
That live
In Him,
Through Her.
They make a Rosary
Of hearts
That beat together
In the same unison of
The little church—
The family that loves God!

And do you know
What God makes
Out of all these hearts?
With a gesture
His hands over the basket—
Or bag—
He makes
A house in heaven,
Just like the one
He lived in on earth—
The first little church
Before the big one
Was born!

And He often visits that house,
With Mary and Joseph
And that is where
She kneels at His feet
And talks to Him
About
This family or that.

That house, made of such hearts,
Is the sixth unknown glory
Of our Lady
In heaven.

For each of these hearts
Beats in unison
With Her heart.
Those are the hearts
Of families
That pray together,
And so stay together—
With Jesus, Mary, and Joseph
In heaven.

The Seventh Glory

B lack,
Nuns' black.
The cape of white.
Virginal white.
The belt, soft leather
Finely wrought,
The feet unshod
Except for sandals—
Very light,
And also finely wrought.
She descends
Most modestly;
With eyes downcast,
And for all to see
A novice is She
That somehow
Seems to have wandered
From behind
Some convent wall.

But there is no one to see
As She passes by.
She came, quite evidently,
To visit convents.
Slowly She wends Her way
And enters
One after the other.
Sometimes She comes out
With a flower in her hand,
Sometimes with none.

The strangest thing is
That you would expect all lilies
From such holy places.
Instead you have
The most astounding variety.
From little humble violets
To roses, dark red
And in full bloom.

Strange too
Is that fact that,
Though She has visited so many convents
The flowers are few.
But those She has
Are full of fragrance
And She seems delighted
To press them
Against Her face
And smell the fragrance
Of them
As She wends Her way
To the next place.

The pilgrimage is long.
There are so many convents.
And it is getting late
In the day.
Still She goes Her way.
And still the bouquet
Is not too big.
True, She needs two hands
To hold in now.
She holds it
In the crook of Her arm,
Her left one—
Next to Her heart.

You'd think that
If She gathers
The fragrant blooms
Of wholly consecrated lives
Lived in Her Son
And to Herself,
She would
Have to call
On angels
And archangels
To carry off the flowers
From within the hallowed walls.
But slender, small,
She carries easily
The bouquet
She has thus far collected.

It isn't small
But it isn't big.
However, She seems pleased
With even as much as that.
Yet we detect
A little shadow—
Or maybe not.
Is it sadness?
Or is it not?
It might be.
We cannot see too well
Beneath the cape of white
That shadows Her eyes
Somewhat.

And now
It is night,
Slowly She ascends
Back whence She came.
Her feet are slower than usual.

However, She moves
With easy grace
Right up to the throne
Of Her Son
And lays the flowers
On His lap.

He picks them up
One by one,
And looks them over
And smells their fragrant smell,
Then lays them down.
He looks at Her,
And She looks back
And smiles a little,
Then He gathers
The flowers
Together,
And gives them back
Into Her outstretched hands.

And lo!
They make a slender band
Around Her finger.
Slender, indeed,
But She looks tender
And kisses it.
This is the seventh unknown glory
Of Our Lady—
The souls of holy nuns
Who go to make up
The slender band
The Queen of Virgins
Wears upon Her hand.

As you well know,
Nuns are wedded to Her Son—

And so is She
Because She is the Spouse
Of the Holy Spirit.
But He is One of Three
Who are Three-in-One,
So She is the Spouse of the Son too!
And the band
Stands
For the mystical marriage
Of the soul
With the Tremendous
And Divine Lover.

So, She who was wooed
By God
Has a right
To the ring
That the Church
Puts on the finger
Of the nun
On her symbolic
Wedding day
When she pronounces
Perpetual vows
Of love and fidelity.
Yes, that is
The seventh unknown glory
Of Our Lady.

But we must pray
That as days follow days
This glory shall be bigger.
For—
For some reason
Hard to understand—
In our days,
It seems
The smallest one.

About the Author

Catherine Kolyschkine was born into an aristocratic family in Russia in 1896, and baptized in the Russian Orthodox Church. Because of her father's work, she grew up in Ukraine, Egypt, and Paris. Many different strands of Christianity were woven into the spiritual fabric of her family background, but it was from the liturgy of the Russian Orthodox Church, the living faith of her father and mother, and the earthy piety of the Russian people themselves that Catherine received the powerful spiritual traditions and symbols of the Christian East.

At fifteen Catherine was married to her first cousin, Boris de Hueck. When World War I broke out, Catherine became a Red Cross nurse at the front, experiencing the horrors of battle firsthand. On her return to St. Petersburg, she and Boris barely escaped with their lives the turmoil of the Russian Revolution, and nearly starved to death as refugees in Finland. They made their way to England where, at the beginning of her new life in the West, Catherine was received into the Catholic Church in 1919.

In 1921 the couple sailed to Canada where, shortly after their arrival in Toronto, Catherine gave birth to their son George. As refugees, they experienced dire poverty for a few years—but soon Catherine's intelligence, energy, and gift for public speaking brought her to the attention of a large lecture bureau. Her talks were popular all across Canada and the United States. Then within a few years, she became an executive with another, international lecture service. She became a North American success story.

In the 1930's, after several years of anguish, Catherine and Boris separated permanently; later the Church annulled their marriage. Prosperous now, Catherine began to feel the promptings of a deeper call through a passage that leaped to her eyes every time she opened the Scriptures: "Arise, go... sell all you possess... take up your cross and follow me." After consulting with the archbishop of the diocese and receiving his blessing, Catherine took a room in a slum section of Toronto and began to quietly love and serve her neighbors, becoming their friend, and praying, hidden in their midst.

Her example of radical Gospel living became a magnet for men and women in search of a way to live their faith. Catherine had not envisaged a community, but when the Archbishop told her that, yes, Christ was calling her to this, she accepted, and soon Friendship House was born. Its works were modest—a shelter for the homeless, meals for the hungry, recreation and books for the young, a newspaper to make known the social teachings of the Church.

In 1938 Catherine initiated an interracial apostolate in Harlem, New York, living with and serving the African-Americans there. This work expanded to other cities: Chicago, Washington, D.C., and Portland, Oregon. Friendship House became well known in the American Church, although, because her approach was so different from what was being done at the time, Catherine encountered much persecution and resistance to her work.

Her second marriage in 1943 to the American journalist Eddie Doherty ignited new conflicts in Friendship House. Catherine resigned as director, and in 1947 she and Eddie retired to the little village of Combermere, in Ontario, Canada. What seemed like the end of the road turned out to be the most fruitful period of Catherine's life. The community of Madonna House was born, and grew into an open family of lay men, lay women, and priests, living in love and breathing from the "two lungs," East and West, of the Catholic Church. Combermere became the seedbed of an apostolate now numbering around 200 staff workers and 125 associate priests, deacons, and bishops, with 17 field-houses located in various countries.

The training center in Combermere, Ontario offers an experience of Gospel life to guests who come to participate fully in the community life. In the Madonna House way of life are the seeds of a new Christian civilization.

As Catherine's inner life deepened and the community matured, she shared the fullness of the inner vocation that Christ had formed in her. Over the years Catherine authored dozens of books; her book *Poustinia: Encountering God in Silence, Solitude and Prayer* is hailed as a modern spiritual classic and has been translated into numerous languages.

Catherine Doherty died on December 14, 1985 at the age of 89. The cause for her canonization is in process and she is officially recognized as a 'Servant of God.'

You can learn more about Catherine Doherty and her cause for canonization at:

http://www.catherinedoherty.org/

You can learn more the Madonna House Apostolate founded by Catherine at:

http://www.madonnahouse.org/

Other Books by Catherine Doherty
Available through Madonna House Publications

Apostolic Farming
Beginning Again: Recovering your innocence through
      Confession
Bogoroditza: She who gave birth to God
Dear Father
Dear Seminarian
Dearly Beloved: Letters to the Children of My Spirit
      (3 Volumes)
Donkey Bells: Advent and Christmas
Experience of God, An
Fragments of My Life
God in the Nitty-Gritty Life
Grace in Every Season
In the Footprints of Loneliness
In the Furnace of Doubts
Light in the Darkness
Listen to the Spirit: Calendar Journal
Little Mandate, The
Living the Gospel without Compromise
Molchanie: The Silence of God
Moments of Grace (perpetual calendar)
My Russian Yesterdays
Not Without Parables
On the Cross of Rejection
People of the Towel and the Water
Poustinia: Encountering God in Silence and Solitude
Season of Mercy: Lent and Easter
Sobornost
Soul of My Soul: Coming to the Heart of Prayer
Stations of the Cross
Strannik: The Call to the Pilgrimage of the Heart
Uródivoi: Holy Fools